SHIPBOARD
STYLE

SHIPBOARD STYLE

COLIN ANDERSON OF THE ORIENT LINE

RUTH ARTMONSKY

For Stella, Becky and Sally, whose very existence keeps me going.

Published by Artsmonsky Arts
Flat 1, 27 Henrietta Street
London WC2E 8NA
ruthartmonsky@yahoo.co.uk
Tel. 020 7240 8774

Text © Ruth Artmonsky 2010

Designed by David Preston Studio
www.davidprestonstudio.com

Printed in England by Empress Litho Ltd.
Dockyard Industrial Estate, Woolwich Church Street
London SE18 5PQ

ISBN 978-0-9551994-6-2

Previous page Colin Anderson. *The Design Archives, University of Brighton*

CONTENTS

INTRODUCTION

Some time ago I put together a small book on Jack Beddington, the publicity manager for Shell-Mex BP in the 1930s. I was intrigued by the fact that, outside a fairly narrow field of interest, few people, nowadays, had heard of him. Yet Beddington had a considerable influence not only on the development of advertising and of documentary film, but as someone, virtually deified by young final-year art students, able to start them out on their careers. I titled the book *Jack Beddington: The Footnote Man*, as no one had thought he merited a book, he merely appeared as a footnote in books on the lives of other people.

I had planned to do a series on other such footnote people – Noel Carrington with Penguin, Peter Gregory at Lund Humphries, Stephen Tallents at the Empire Marketing Board and the Post Office, and so on. High on my list was Colin Anderson, now even less known than Beddington. Yet Anderson, by his considerable practical intelligence, his energy and enthusiasm, his diligence, his amiability and diplomacy, not only radically altered the interior design of Britain's ocean liners afloat, but, by his willingness for public service, he was to exert a further influence on art and design ashore through his membership, frequently chairmanship, of myriad governmental and voluntary organisations.

A small display of liners' interiors at the Victoria & Albert Museum in 2009 declared that: 'Ocean Liner interior design has been little examined by comparison to the construction and external design of these great ships.' This encouraged me to use Anderson's contribution as a vehicle to partly redress the neglect inferred, as well as to salute his wider contribution to the Arts.

COLIN ANDERSON

OF THE ORIENT LINE

David Ogilvy, whose advertising agency was used by Colin Anderson, claimed that he was their only client who could Scottish dance as well as embroider. This could immediately bring to mind an eccentric, a term his friend Kenneth Clark occasionally applied to him. But 'unpicking' the two activities is essential to understanding the two major elements to Anderson, for his Scottish shipping lineage marked out his career, and a strong aesthetic sensitivity determined the role he carved out for himself within his career.

James Thompson & Co., Scottish shipbrokers, was established in 1797, and owned a small fleet of sailing ships. The Andersons enter the picture when, in 1854, James George Anderson, a relation, joined the firm. By 1863 the surname Anderson joined that of Thompson when the company became Anderson, Thompson & Co.; and, with the death of the last Thompson in 1869, the name was changed, yet again, to Anderson, Anderson & Co.

In 1866 the company started a shipping service to Australia that traded under the name The Orient Line of Packets, shortened to the Orient Line. The Green family joined the Andersons, jointly forming the Orient Steam Navigation Company, which commissioned its first steamer – the *Orient* in 1879. (Sir Kenneth Anderson and Sir Frederick Green were to alternate annually as Orient Line chairman.) Growth was such that five new Orient Line ships joined their fleet in 1909 – *Otway*, *Osterley*, *Orsova*, *Otranto* and *Orvieto*. The Orient Line had decided to have all their boats' names starting with 'O' (as Cunard was to have all theirs ending in 'ia'). This may have helped to simplify liner recognition, but the waters were muddied by the Orient Line sometimes giving new boats the name of defunct boats, with a Roman numeral added to indicate how many previous boats had held that name, for example, *Orcades III*.

At the turn of the century the Orient Line developed an association with the Peninsular & Oriental Steam Navigation Company (P&O), as the two companies shared the Australian government mail contract. By 1919 P&O had a controlling interest in the Orient Line when Green sold them his shares and Anderson, Green & Co. then managed the Orient Line boats for P&O

Elizabeth Garrett Anderson, first woman doctor, first woman mayor and Colin Anderson's grandmother.
National Portrait Gallery

until the companies merged completely in 1960. Such was Colin Anderson's shipping heritage that he was to follow the conventional career path of middle class families of the time – public school (Eton) to university (Trinity College, Oxford) into the family firm.

In addition to shipping, the Andersons had tended to add 'public service' to their curriculum. Not only did Anderson's father take on such responsibilities (including being a founder member and a chairman of the Design & Industry Association in 1915), his grandmother, Dr. Elizabeth Garrett Anderson, whose father had built the Maltings at Snape and whose Suffolk home Anderson visited frequently as a child, provided a remarkable role model for him. She was the first woman to qualify as a doctor, and also became the Mayor of Aldeburgh, the first female mayor. Anderson was to trace his artistic interests back to his childhood collecting of patterned pebbles from the Aldeburgh beach when staying with her.

In Anderson's small book of writings, *Three Score Years and Ten* (1974), Anderson suggests that even as a child he felt rather apart from other children and managed to develop a congenial acceptable façade to mask this. Of Aldeburgh days he penned:

Brisk Aldeburgh ladies asked in
to soften the edge of our screams,
'Where's Colin? Col! Colin!!' they called,
'What a shy little person that seems'.[1]

And, later, of his time at Oxford:

I shot with my short-barrelled Churchills;
I wore a pink coat to the hunt;
I parted my hair in the middle;
and favoured myself in a punt.[2]

Sir Kenneth Clark, Anderson's mentor and friend. *National Portrait Gallery*

Yet he recorded of his time at Oxford: 'I was outwardly as muddy as any other oaf. I kept my aesthetic core carefully hidden, just as I do today; but I suppose a chink must have shown.' The 'chink' could well have been exposed on Anderson meeting up with a fellow student, Kenneth Clark, who, although a year his senior, had an adjoining room. Clark, who was to become a lifelong friend, provided a model for Anderson that aestheticism was not only acceptable, but admirable. Anderson wrote of the shock he felt when first seeing how Clark had furnished his college rooms:

> The pictures were actually real, and there wasn't a Medici print to be seen. The College furniture had somehow been neutralised. There were precious-looking, breakable objects in vulnerable profusion. A large new-fangled gramophone, without a horn, played not 'Tea for Two' or 'Kitten on the Keys', but the works of people like … Bartok.[3]

Clark was to claim that he and Anderson were to have had a continuous friendship from their Oxford days but, in fact, they lost contact with each other, and it was only when the Clarks bumped into the Andersons, wheeling their first child in its pram by the Round Pond (Colin had married Morna MacCormick, an Australian, in 1932), that they became really close lifelong friends. Whereas at Oxford Clark's aesthetic influence on Anderson was rather by an unconscious osmosis, from 1932 onwards the influence was direct. Through Clark, Anderson was to meet the likes of John Piper, Graham Sutherland and Henry Moore, and many other young artists who he was to commission and whose works he collected. Clark was at the centre of the London art scene and was to act as Anderson's guide and mentor thenceforth. When Anderson knew he was dying he wrote to Clark that he was the friend to whom he owed more pleasure, instruction and hospitality than any that he had had through his life.

The young married Andersons were already adventuring into Modernism, having bought their first house in Kingston, where they had inherited Moorish arches and a pink ceiling with blue clouds. Anderson later wrote in the catalogue for 'The Anderson Collection of Art Nouveau': 'this we despised, for I, at any rate, was already a modern, a contemporary, which at that date was to be a member of an austere caste'. White walls and tubular furniture, mainly commissioned from Heals, soon replaced the Middle Eastern scene.

Anderson was describing himself as 'modern' in contrast to what can only be termed 'historic', at least as far as the interiors of boats were concerned. Anderson had left Oxford in 1925 and by 1930 had become a junior director. He was beginning to take an active interest in the interiors of the Orient Line boats and was determined to bring to them the 'modernism' that he had chosen for his own home. He wrote of his campaign:

> … by the end of the twenties my voice [raised, I expect. All too often out of turn] was producing ripples of disquiet in the Pond of Power, and by 1930 the argument that we must have a clearly contemporary design for the new ship then being contemplated was not only listened to but accepted.[4]

The ship was the *Orion*. The ship itself was to cause a stir, being one-funnelled, with a single mast, and sporting a new colour scheme of corn-colour and green. It also caught the headlines in that it was launched by wireless – the Duke of Gloucester pushing a button in Brisbane while the boat slipped down the runway into Barrow dock. But it was *Orion's* interior that was to have the greater impact.

The Board, although agreeing to 'modernisation', did not feel capable of applying Anderson's ideas themselves, and threw down the gauntlet to him to translate his broad plans into specifics for the boat. Anderson fully appreciated the courage of the Board's decision, for he was totally inexperienced in design and the ship was to cost over one million pounds. Yet such was the strength of Anderson's conviction and evangelism that he showed no hesitation in getting down to his assignment.

It is perhaps more zeitgeist, than by a direct link, that at about the same time, another young man, Jack Beddington, as inexperienced as Anderson in matters of design, was arguing for a more modern approach for Shell-Mex BP publicity and, likewise, was told to put his muscle where his mouth was.

THE 'HISTORIC' LINERS

To appreciate the radical nature of what Anderson achieved with the *Orion* it is necessary to appreciate what was, to him, the enormity of the 'historical'. The Orient Line and P&O (organisationally intertwined from 1920) had worked out a mutually beneficial way of sharing the Australian/Far eastern route. They seem to have adjudged their regular passengers – civil servants, missionaries, émigrés and the like – as meriting reasonably comfortable quarters, but nothing more.

The Atlantic route was another matter. For this there was not only competition between British shipping lines but between nations. The British, along with the French, German, Italians and Scandinavians, were all leap-frogging each other as to who ruled these particular waves, criteria for supremacy being a matter of size, speed and splendour. By the early years of the 20th century the British were in the race with Cunard's *Lusitania*, *Mauretania* and *Aquitania* and White Star's *Titanic*, *Olympic* and *Britannic*. But these were facing the European competition from such boats as Norddeutscher Lloyd's *Kaisser-Wilhelm der Grosse*, *Imperator* and *Vaterland*, and Hamburg-Amerkanische Packetfahrt-Gerellschaft's (HAPAG) *Amerika*.

For steamships up to the *fin-de-siècle*, it was usual practice for the ship owner merely to rely on the shipbuilder to put forward a decorative scheme for a new boat, and this was frequently carried out by local craftsmen or ordered in bulk from what was available from relevant manufacturers, such as Waring & Gillow, Maples, Wylie & Lockhead of Glasgow and Martyns of Cheltenham. Anderson referred to such suppliers as providing 'upholsterart'. This was particularly true of liners built at Harland & Wolff, who, as late as the 1920s, were supplied by Ashby Tabb of Heaton Tabb, an 'historic' man through and through, who abhorred Modernism. The last two White Star liners, *Britannic* (1930) and *Georgic* (1932), were still largely 'period'.

However, when boats became a matter of national pride the Edwardian shipping magnates began to employ architects in their attempts to become the line offering the greatest opulence, albeit shipping directors and their families

Main Staircase, Olympic. *Art & Heritage Services, Southampton*

proffered ideas, largely along the lines of how they would furnish their own grand houses. From the Hon. Elsie Mackay, daughter of P&O's chairman in the 1920s (whose only qualifications were that she had been in films and could fly a plane), to Lady Brocklebank, wife of Cunard's chairman in the 1960s (whose claim was that she was an experienced liner voyager), family interference continued.

Nevertheless, increasing professionalism of design aboard, in the 20th century, paralleled the increasing status of design ashore, with the founding of the Design and Industries Council in 1915, the inauguration of the Society of Industrial Artists in the 1930s, the Board of Trade setting up its National Register of Industrial Art Designers (1936), the RSA establishing its elite Royal Designer for Industry (1936), and the triumphant establishment of the Council of Industrial Design in 1944.

Colin Anderson took some pride in the Orient Line being one of the first shipping companies to commission a professional. He appreciated his grandfather, father and their cousins, being men of some taste, but he had only scathing comments to make on J.J. Stevenson, also a relative, who had been appointed the first of his line's interior designers. Stevenson had done his apprenticeship in the office of Sir Gilbert Scott and was commissioned for the *Orient*, the first of the line's new boats in the 20th century. There would seem to be just the merest thread of glee in Anderson's description of the tendency of Stevenson's heavy decorative ceiling tiles to drop off in rough weather, necessitating the stretching of a net underneath. Stevenson was replaced by Andrew N. Prentice, whose style, Anderson, with similar disdain, described as 'Palladio-Adamesque'.

Alan Powers, in his review of the 'Art on Liners' exhibition at Southampton Art Gallery (1986), with one sweep of the pen, wrote off the Edwardian liners as far as design was concerned:

When the *Titanic* sank in 1912 there was no cause to mourn the lost works of art on board for liners of the Edwardian era did their best to resemble rather stuffy country house interiors carried out by high-class decorators.[5]

Certainly it seems curious, in hindsight, that boats that were broadcast as the most advanced technically should not also have led the way when it came to their interiors. Anderson, in panning Prentice's designs, declared

Opposite
Title page for passenger guide book featuring Kate Greenaway border design, 1890.

Right
Dining Saloon, early Orient Line liner.

First Class stairwell, Aquitania [Panini oil]. *Art & Heritage Services, Southampton*

that not only were they not modern, but that even Art Nouveau had escaped him. The Edwardian designers of ship's interiors were intent not only to cocoon passengers from any hint that they were at sea, but from any hint of 'contemporary', let alone avant-garde, that might be on the scene ashore.

From the *Lusitania* and *Aquitania* of around 1907, to the *Olympic* and *Titanic* (1911–14), shipping lines set out to reproduce, as accurately as possible, the grandest of European interiors of the 17th and 18th centuries, abounding with panelling, fireplaces, stained glass domes, damask, velvets, tapestries and gilded frames. These were not merely pastiche but were often meticulously researched designs, sometimes actually including original objects and paintings of the period being used. The first class Jacobean drawing room of the *Titanic* was based on designs for Hatton Hall; the mahogany tables of the *Aquitania's* drawing room were taken from drawings for ones at Sion House; the first class dining room of the *Olympic* used plans for Hatfield House; while an adaptation of the old Greenwich Hospital during the Restoration period inspired the Carolean smoking room of the *Aquitania*; and so on.

Many of the boats included rooms of more than one period. The *Titanic* drew from William and Mary, Jacobean, Georgian and Louis XIV; and the *Aquitania* focused on the period between the Restoration and the end of the 18th century. Perhaps the ultimate in pretentiousness were the best suites aboard the *Aquitania*, variously named Van Dyke, Holbein, Velasquez, Rembrandt, Romney, Raeburn, Gainsborough and Reynolds, and decorated accordingly.

Wood abounded and oak was predominant, festooned with carvings à la Grinley Gibbons, the frames of tables resplendent with female figures, the walls smothered with boisseries. Textiles tended to be tapestry, needlepoint and damask. Wrought iron, particularly for balustrades, was intricately worked with flowers. Several of the early British liners employed the Bromsgrove Guild for this. Based on the Bromsgrove and Birmingham Schools of Art, the Guild was founded in 1898 and had provided decorations for P&O *Moldavia* (1903) before producing their finest metalwork for the bronze and glass lift

enclosure and staircase, spanning five decks of the *Lusitania*. For the Orient Line *Orvieto* and *Obama*, in addition to metalwork, the Guild provided stained glass and plaster ceilings, of which Sir Kenneth, Anderson's father, was particularly proud. Even when boats had to be refitted, after their service in the First World War, there seemed no reason to change things. As late as the 1930s White Star's *Britannic* was still sporting the 'historic' style.

The British ship owners were not only alert to what was happening with their European competitor's liner interiors, they were also eager to employ the same designers. Particular interest was shown in the work of the partnership

28

Corner of Saloon, Mauretania.
*Art & Heritage Services,
Southampton*

of Mewes and Davis that Albert Ballin of HAPAG had come across when dining at the Ritz Carlton Grill, and was using for the public rooms of his new liner *Amerika*. Ernest Cunard was determined to use them for his own expanding fleet, and because of possible conflict of interest contractual haggles were long drawn out. Eventually, Davis was to become Cunard's man for the *Aquitania* and was still contributing, in the 1930s, to the designs for the *Queen Mary*.

Davis had originally been inclined to take a more modern stance on interior design but was persuaded, or rather resigned himself, to Cunard's enthusiasm for hotel opulence.

> The first day out, I enjoyed the beautiful sea, but when we got well on to the Atlantic there was one thing I craved for as never before, and that was a warm fire and a pink shade. I suggest to you that the transatlantic liner is not merely a ship, she is a floating town with 3,000 passengers of all kinds, with all sorts of tastes, and those who enjoy being there are distinctly in the minority. If we could get ships to look like ships, and get people to enjoy the sea, it would be a very good thing, but all we can do, as things are, is to give them gigantic floating hotels.[6]

And so, by the 1920s and 30s, when hotels were adopting the glitz, glamour and sophistication of Art Deco, shipping lines were echoing this with the opulence of the *Normandie* and the *Queen Mary*. Colin Anderson was to take an altogether different route.

THE 'ORION' AND 'ORCADES II'

In criticising Prentice's work for the Orient Line, Anderson wrote:

> Andrew Prentice never betrayed any knowledge of the existence of the Bauhaus or Dudok or indeed of anything that could seriously be described as new style.[7]

Although this is possibly Anderson's sole use of the word 'Bauhaus' Veronika Sekules, quoting from unpublished papers, stressed his admiration of Bauhaus ideas, and described him as being 'extremely informed about contemporary architecture and design'. The Bauhaus, intent on social and political reform, had an altogether more Puritanical attitude to design than Art Deco devotees. Gropius, in the Bauhaus Manifesto put out in 1919 on the founding of the school, declared:

> Let us create a new guild of craftsmen, without class distinctions which raise an arrogant barrier between craftsman and artist, together let us conceive and create the new building of the future, which will embrace architecture and sculpture and painting in a single unity, and which will rise one day towards the heaven from the hands of a million workers like the crystal symbol of a new faith.[8]

Anderson certainly saw himself as a 'rebel' in his battle against the 'historic' style, but could have had little real understanding or sympathy with such aims. What Anderson took from the Bauhaus movement, watered down to an Anglicised acceptability, was firstly its complete break with swagger and showiness, and secondly its harnessing of technology to provide simple, undecorated, essentially functional design; 'fitness for purpose' became his motto. Rather than compare liners to 'floating hotels' Anderson described them as 'unusually mobile public vehicles' and for him 'high' style was totally 'inappropriate for purpose'.

In setting out to apply his own ideas Anderson saw as his primary task the necessity to search out an architect or designer who would be in sympathy.

The main staircase, Ashcombe Tower
designed by Brian O'Rorke 1933–36.

Sorting through photographs he gave serious consideration to such modernists as Edward Maufe, Oliver Hill, Serge Chermayeff and Wells Coates. Although admiring their work, Anderson was apprehensive about his ability, young and inexperienced as he was, to manage such well-established names. There are several versions of how Anderson came upon Brian O'Rorke. He himself wrote that it was from photographs, but it is more than likely that he had been influenced in his choice of O'Rorke by seeing his work at the house of his friends, Betty and Ralph Rayner, which O'Rorke had built and furnished in a modern, functional way.

O'Rorke, a New Zealander, had trained at Jesus College, Cambridge University and at the Architectural Association School in London, and was definitely a modernist. Of much the same age as Anderson, O'Rorke was building up a reputation for himself, initially with private clients. It was his work for the Mayor Gallery in Cork Street that was to give him a wider publicity. Fred Mayor had gone into partnership with James Duthie and Douglas Cooper, with the aim of showing the most progressive contemporary artists in thoroughly modern surroundings.

Barbara Wadsworth, writing of her father Edward's exhibition in the gallery in 1933, described the sensation that O'Rorke had achieved:

> Gone were the soft velvet curtains and damask panels, the stained woodwork and the gilded lights clipped to the top of each picture frame. Gone too was the atmosphere of 'Hush! You are in a Prescence! ... at 18 Cork Street all was light, light, light. The walls were white and without cornices to the ceilings, there were cross-set partitions to provide extra hanging space and steel-framed furniture!'[9]

This chimed in exactly with what Anderson had in mind for the new ship. Once he and O'Rorke had got together, they discovered not only shared aesthetic values, but also a similar conscientious, meticulous working approach. Anderson had no idea of being a sleeping partner and the pair were to work

in harmony not only for the *Orion* but for all subsequent Orient Line boats, including its last, the *Oriana*. O'Rorke was a quiet and rather scholarly man, uninvolved in professional politics and ambitions, yet well able to hold his own in the partnership. Anderson seems to have been able, by tact and diplomacy, to have given O'Rorke a sufficient creative freedom, yet was able to oversee every step of any project to his own satisfaction.

Providing graphics for Anderson in the 1950s and 60s, Dorrit Dekk gave a picture of Anderson's typical relationship with his designer on any project – absolute urbanity; clear definition of task; abundant flowing of visual ideas to and fro; no rejections but rather, 'Have you considered such and such a possibility?'; and an efficient focus – what, where, by when? By Anderson's

Right
O'Rorke drawings for Dance
Floor of the Orion.
RIBA Library Drawings Collection

Opposite
O'Rorke, detail of Lounge, Orion.
RIBA Library Drawings Collection

patronage O'Rorke could work without the publicity, and consequent restraint, that designers for government-subsidized boats just could not have.

The only aspect they seem to have had any major difference on was whether curtains were 'modern'. Anderson was anti-curtains, as potential gatherers of dust and preventers of ventilation, but O'Rorke argued his corner and eventually curtains were accepted where their functionality could be proved.

Vickers of Barrow-in-Furness had been commissioned to build the *Orion*. Anderson thought himself lucky in that their reputation had largely been achieved by naval projects and they had little experience of ocean liners. To Anderson, that meant that they might not be prejudiced by traditional practice, and that this would make for an easier working relationship.

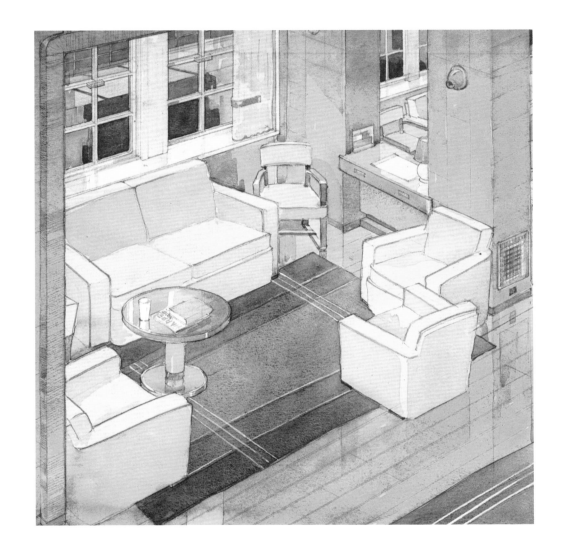

In October 1933 Anderson drew up a rough-and-ready brief for O'Rorke –
no period decorations but no extremity of Modernism; the importance of
such functional considerations as extreme weather conditions; the commercial
requirement of maximum seating capacity in the public rooms, appropriately
lit; accident prevention of non-slip flooring; fire-resistant materials; low
maintenance of all surfaces and furnishings; and versatility of room usage.

When the pair got down to Bills of Quantities their obsessional natures
led to reams of foolscap, the effect of which Anderson described as:

> … almost Proustian in its appraisal of the qualities expected … I have
> been assured that there were moments when this meticulous attention
> to what seemed unimportant attention to detail [for instance in the
> placing of cabin shelves and hooks] brought the responsible officials
> of the shipbuilders near the breaking point.[10]

Although the term 'ergonomics' had yet to be coined, much of their time was
to be spent on measuring and market research, down to the size and number
of toiletries carried by male and female passengers respectively, and how these
were handled on a voyage.

However, the major problem facing Anderson and O'Rorke was not so
much what was needed, as where to find sufficiently modern suppliers:

> It would be hard to exaggerate the difficulties we met in the prevailing
> proud and successful industries, that not a single object of their entire
> output was acceptable for a modern ship interior. How could we
> explain even what we meant by such an interior? We found ourselves
> having to discover designers capable of producing new designs for a
> wide range of products from carpets to cutlery who understood what
> we were after. And this was not at all easy, for there were no such
> people as industrial designers; there were a few artist designers,
> if one knew where to find them.[11]

SS ORION 1935

THE NEW 23.371 TON ORIENT LINER

ROOM TO SWING A TIGER

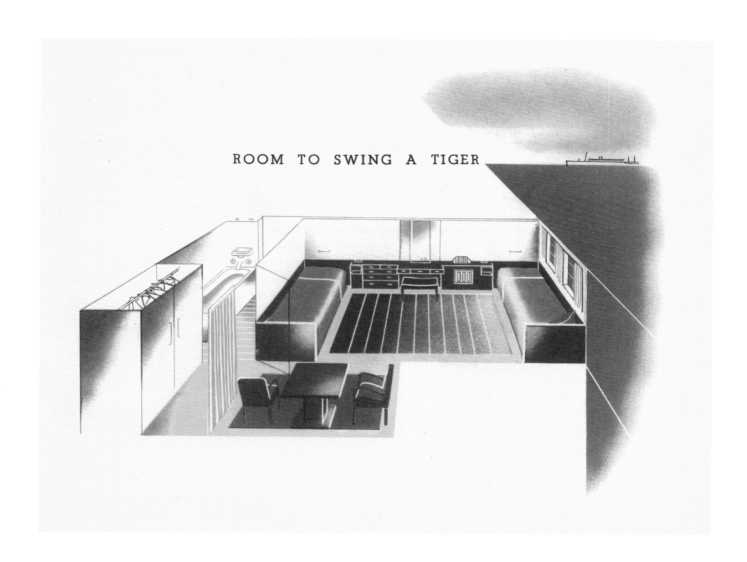

SUN, AIR AND EXERCISE

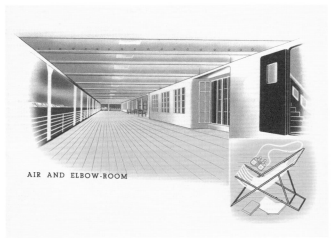

AIR AND ELBOW-ROOM

A PLACE IN THE SUN

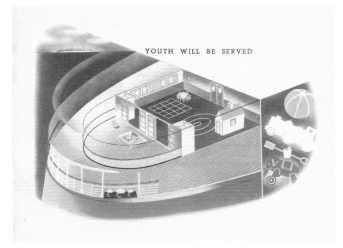

YOUTH WILL BE SERVED

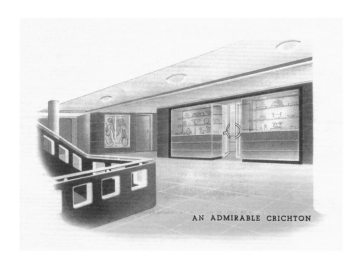

AN ADMIRABLE CRICHTON

ALL THAT YOU NEED

COMFORT AND DIGNITY

A ROOM WITH A VIEW

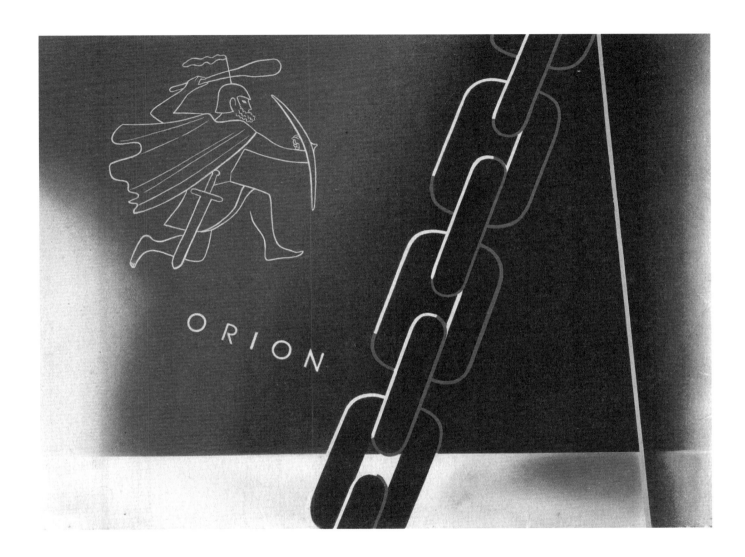

ORION

Tourist Class Café, Orion. *P&O Archives*

First Class Tavern, Orion. *P&O Archives*

It fell on Anderson's shoulders to persuade manufacturers to supply their needs, not only in matters of 'look', but in sufficiently large numbers for the boat. For example, it was Anderson who persuaded Whitefriars to produce Keith Murray's glassware designs, and Wedgwood to supply his china.

Almost all of the furnishings for the *Orion* had to be specially designed and made for the boat. O'Rorke was to design a good deal of the furniture himself. Lynton Lamb (now better remembered for his book design and illustration) was called on for the ship's badge and engraved mirrors for the first class lounge; Tristram Hillier provided an internally lit mural for the first class café; Gordon Russell (to run the Utility Scheme in the Second World War and to be the first director of the Council of Industrial Design) did some of the library fittings; Edward Bawden and Keith Murray were responsible for much of the china and Murray for the glass; even Mrs O'Rorke was drawn in to design decorative lighting. The young Ceri Richards, then recorded by his middle name of Giraldus, was curiously employed on designing floor inlays as well as a coloured brochure. He was to become a great favourite of Anderson's, who bought his paintings and commissioned him for subsequent boats.

Much of the textiles used for the tourist class were from Sheila Walsh and Allan Walton. Allan Walton, and his brother Robert, ran Allan Walton Textiles, London. The firm was considered one of the most advanced. Allan not only designed himself, but also commissioned some of the best-known artists of the time, including Vanessa Bell, Duncan Grant and Frank Dobson.

By far the most important textile designer used, as far as Anderson was concerned, was Marion Dorn, and this was to be the first sea-going use of her work. An American, she had accompanied her partner, Edward McKnight Kauffer, when he decided to relocate to London in 1923. By 1928 Dorn was providing designs for the Royal Wilton Carpet Factory, for the Midland Hotel in Morecombe and for Claridges, as well as furnishings for the rich and famous, for example, interiors for Arnold Bennett's flat. By 1929 Dorn and McKnight Kauffer had an exhibition of their work at Arthur Tooth's Gallery, which was

Below
Luggage label by McKnight Kauffer.

Right
'Orient Line Cruises' poster by
Edward McKnight Kauffer.
P&O Archives

showing such modernists as Wadsworth. Her designs tended to have natural backgrounds with strong geometrical lines or abstract forms, all in muted tones, influenced by Cubism and the work of Sonia Delaunay. She had already provided rugs for a private home that O'Rorke was developing.

As Dorn's work was expensive, Anderson only used her for the first class accommodation of the *Orion* – the library, lounge, the galleries and around the dance floor; and, of course, in the State Room. Although her work was generally admired, Geoffrey Grigson, in *The Studio*, was a lone voice finding her carpeting 'irritatingly confused'. A more typical opinion was that given in an article in *Shipbuilding and Shipping Record*:

> Looking for the first time at a newly completed apartment it is always interesting to speculate about what originally inspired the designer – which item came first and how was the decorative scheme built up? In this particular instance there can be no doubt whatever that a basis was first provided by the Dorn rugs, for upon them everything else hinges. No setting other than the plain walls could do justice to these fine rugs.[12]

McKnight Kauffer was commissioned to provide an engraved mirror for the first class dining saloon. This was of immense proportions (9ft x 13ft) and portrayed the giant *Orion*. He also produced a range of graphics for Anderson – invitations, posters and, particularly striking, tie-on labels in luminous raspberry and pink or lime and black. Dorn and McKnight Kauffer became close friends of the Andersons'. Anderson later wrote of McKnight Kauffer:

> Ted Kauffer was a pleasure to the eye even without bringing into play his other pleasing characteristics. Cultured, intelligent and hypersensitive, his fastidiousness eternally governed his surroundings, his comings and goings, and his choice of company.

NEW ORIENT LINER

ORION

TOURIST

Opposite
'New Orient Line' brochure cover
designed by Edward McKnight Kauffer.
National Maritime Museum,
Greenwich

Above
McKnight Kauffer china for the Orient Line.
Photo Peter Harpley

ORIENT LINE TO AUSTRALIA

INFORMATION FOR PASSENGERS

Opposite
McKnight Kauffer china for the Orient Line.
National Maritime Museum, Greenwich

Left
Orient Line to Australia brochure cover
featuring McKnight Kauffer logo design.

One cannot remember anything that he produced which hadn't the quality of orderliness and it was this, added to the brilliance of his basic conceptions which made the impact of his work so dynamic.[13]

Both Dorn and McKnight Kauffer were given commissions for later Orient liners, and Dorn also supplied rugs for Cunard's *Queen Mary*. They returned to America in 1940 and Anderson penned them a poem 'For Two Friends who are missed'. In 1941 he sent Dorn a further one – 'For a Frustrated American Textile Designer Whose Clients insist on Roses':

I know a Bank where wild roses bloom;
a down-town Bank with air-conditioned rooms;
a Bank whose President feels socially uncertain
without any roses rambling up his curtain.
I ask what sort of rose he would prefer?
'A Bourbon rose' he says 'without demur.'[14]

Anderson was sure that the *Orion* would have been a far more provincial boat without the pair. He admitted to relying on McKnight Kauffer for 'personal encouragement and much general draughtsmanship, design know-how and typographic advice', albeit allowing that it was O'Rorke's hand on the *Orion* that really made the boat such a success and set the pattern for subsequent Orient liners; in architectural circles the *Orion* came to be referred to as the 'O'Rorke'.

Anderson and O'Rorke were in harness not only for the *Orion's* furniture and furnishings; by getting involved early on in the construction of the boat, they were also able to influence its internal structuring. No longer were there to be walled-off rooms for smoking, letter writing, ladies withdrawing and such like. The public rooms of the *Orion*, and subsequent Orient Line boats, became more like open spaces flowing into each other, and these spaces became more versatile in the functions they provided at different times of the day and night

Passageway of the Orion. *Photographic Archives, Merseyside Maritime Museum*

Staircase of the Orion. *Photographic Archives, Merseyside Maritime Museum*

Marion Dorn Rugs, First Class Gallery,
Orion. *P&O Archives*

and for different events. For the *Orion*, Dorn's rugs and carpets aided any demarcation necessary.

The publicity brochure for the *Orion*, illustrated by Ceri Richards, described the boat as 'the reflection of the age in which she serves the public … a ship stripped of unwanted frills, beautiful by being fitted for her purpose'. Anderson and O'Rorke had produced the first genuinely contemporary British liner. *Orion* was not only 'contemporary' but 'co-ordinated', in that every decoration and artefact, down to publicity material, menus, ship's information and the steward's buttons, had the same stylistic design. Anderson felt that if the *Orion* had been ahead of taste when she came into service, she would end her life abreast of it.

Anderson's contribution to the project, and to the subsequent Orient Line boats, is well caught by David McKee, one of the later Line's naval architects:

> … he was prepared to spend considerable time on the drawing board not only in concepts but on details of design, whether the design was related to the décor of the ships or to some practical matter. I found him very knowledgeable indeed about how every part of the ship worked, or was expected to work, to give the best results. He was obviously a very acute observer of everything that went on on board and able to apply that ability to the improvement of all aspects of design.[15]

Anderson and O'Rorke's next venture, *Orcades II*, launched in 1937, was a short-lived ship as it was sunk, on war service, some five years later. Its interior design was much along the same lines as the *Orion*, using many of the same designers – Dorn again for rugs for first class rooms, Lynton Lamb for the ship's badge and an engraved mirror, and Ceri Richards for an imposing wood, steel and glass bas relief – 'Neptune watching the course of a ship' – considered something of a conversation piece for the first class dining room. And again the brochure stressed Anderson's values of simplicity and functionality:

Edward Bawden crockery in 'Heartsease' pattern for the Orient Line. *P&O Archives*

> The design and decoration have been shorn of unneeded extravagance. There is nothing more tempting in decorating a ship than to gain effect by mere magnificence. Passengers admire it at the outset, but on a voyage something smaller and more 'easy to live in' is needed.[16]

Having established an effective working relationship with Vickers, Anderson and O'Rorke had earned enough brownie points to become involved at an early stage in the naval architecture of *Orcades II*, and this enabled them to build on their opening up of public spaces for versatility of usage, that had started on the *Orion*. Additionally, first class passengers on the *Orion* had hoped for better vistas, and with the *Orcades II* Anderson and O'Rorke achieved greatly enlarged windows in the first class lounge which were much appreciated.

Orcades II also started the trend of the Orient Line to use artists and designers from overseas, particularly from Australasia, the destination of the company's boats. John Hutton, a New Zealander, was commissioned for a mural, *The Orkneys*, for the tourist café; and Margaret Preston, an Australian, did flower-paintings, which hung in the first class café.

A footnote to the *Orcades II* was O'Rorke refusing a design for a painted dome from Graham Sutherland, news that Anderson received with horror, as Sutherland was a favourite. As with the 'curtains' episode, that the issue was seen as 'necessary conflict' indicates the strength of their working relationship, and again Anderson deferred to O'Rorke's professional judgement. In a lecture to the Royal Society of Arts Anderson defined their respective roles as he saw them:

> The importance of removing all responsibility from the client's Board as a whole for choosing and approving decorative schemes can scarcely be over-stressed. The interior design of ships calls for professionals, just as much as navigation and catering do, but the member of the Board who presides over the Design Committee *is* a

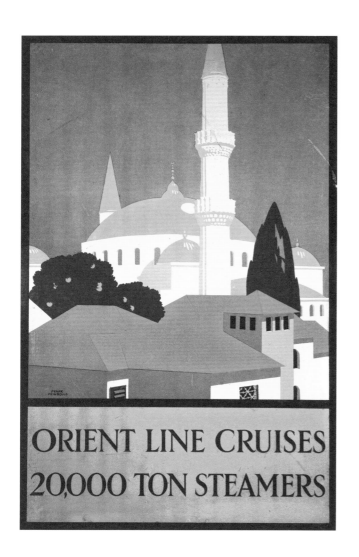

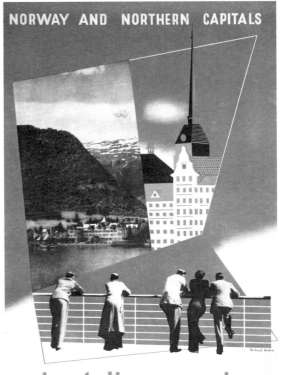

Orient line china with compass motif. *National Maritime Museum, Greenwich*

professional. He represents the people who are paying for the ship in the first instance, and who seek to make her pay thereafter. All he has to remember is that, though he is a professional ship owner, he is not a professional designer as well. And the same, but in reverse, goes for those who are.[17]

The understatement of the design for these pre-war Orient Line boats is to be compared with the glitzy show of the *Queen Mary*, which although commissioned before them in 1931, due to economic circumstances had its maiden voyage after them. The *Queen Mary*, seen to be the British answer to the French *Normandie*, like it, took the Art Deco route. Sir Percy Bates, Cunard's chairman, chose an American designer, Benjamin Morris, to get a more transatlantic viewpoint. The *Orion's* restraint – plain surfaces, smooth columns, concealed lighting, muted colours – compared tastefully with the magnificence supplied for the American traveller. Clive Bell, the art critic, provided a cutting criticism of the *Queen* in *The Listener*:

> What the management wants, and gets, is the humouristic-artistic. That is the prevailing note. The Teddy Bear Style. Nothing is suffered to be merely good-looking, it must be funny as well, which means that barely anything is good-looking and that almost everything is vulgar ... The decoration of the *Queen Mary* is facetious.[18]

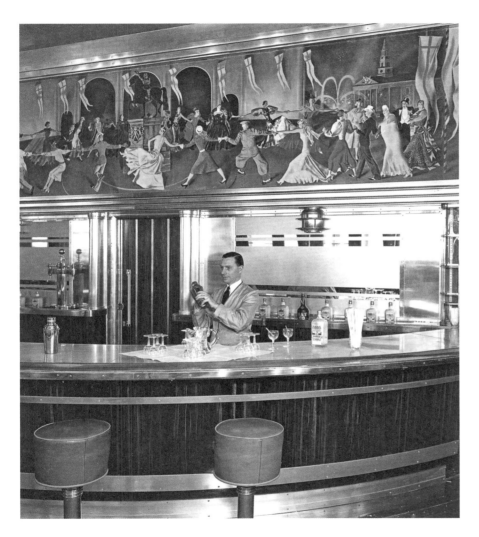

Left
First Class Lounge of the Orcades II
with John Armstrong mural and
Marion Dorn carpet. *RIBA Library,
Photographs Collection*

Opposite
Ceri Richards wall decoration, First
Class Dining Salon, Orcades II.
RIBA Library, Photographs Collection

Marion Dorn carpet, Library, Orcades II. *RIBA Library, Photographs Collection*

This page
Lynton Lamb, engraved mirror,
First Class Restaurant of the Orion.

RIBA Library, Photographs Collection

P&O Archives

Left
Leo Felton light fitting, First Class
Dining Salon, Orion. *RIBA Library,
Photographs Collection*

Opposite
Menu Covers [artist unknown but in
the style of Claude Flight School].

73

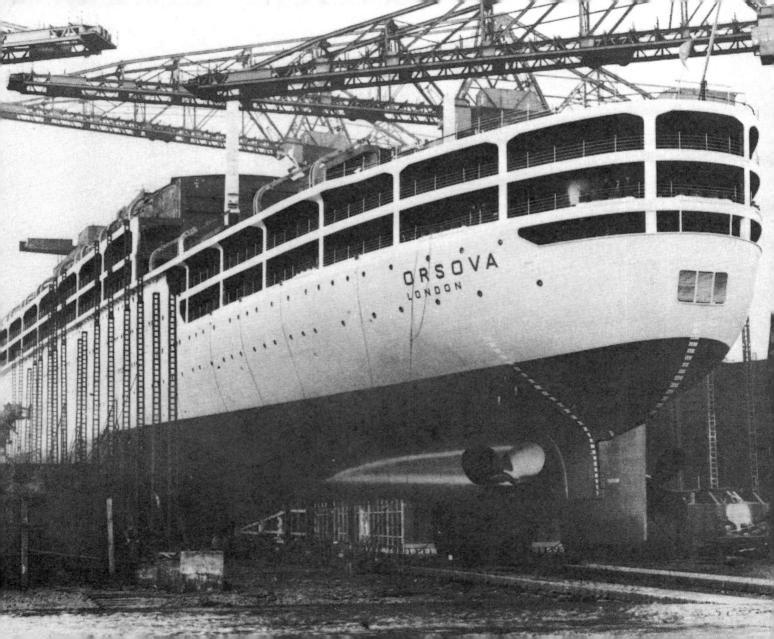

POST-WAR ORIENT LINE LINERS

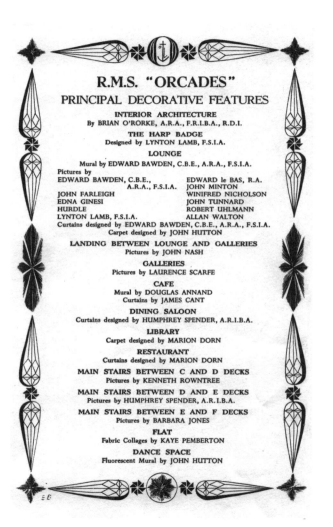

R.M.S. "ORCADES"
PRINCIPAL DECORATIVE FEATURES

INTERIOR ARCHITECTURE
By BRIAN O'RORKE, A.R.A., F.R.I.B.A., R.D.I.

THE HARP BADGE
Designed by LYNTON LAMB, F.S.I.A.

LOUNGE
Mural by EDWARD BAWDEN, C.B.E., A.R.A., F.S.I.A.

Pictures by

EDWARD BAWDEN, C.B.E., A.R.A., F.S.I.A.	EDWARD le BAS, R.A.
	JOHN MINTON
JOHN FARLEIGH	WINIFRED NICHOLSON
EDNA GINESI	JOHN TUNNARD
HURDLE	ROBERT UHLMANN
LYNTON LAMB, F.S.I.A.	ALLAN WALTON

Curtains designed by EDWARD BAWDEN, C.B.E., A.R.A., F.S.I.A.
Carpet designed by JOHN HUTTON

LANDING BETWEEN LOUNGE AND GALLERIES
Pictures by JOHN NASH

GALLERIES
Pictures by LAURENCE SCARFE

CAFE
Mural by DOUGLAS ANNAND
Curtains by JAMES CANT

DINING SALOON
Curtains designed by HUMPHREY SPENDER, A.R.I.B.A.

LIBRARY
Carpet designed by MARION DORN

RESTAURANT
Curtains designed by MARION DORN

MAIN STAIRS BETWEEN C AND D DECKS
Pictures by KENNETH ROWNTREE

MAIN STAIRS BETWEEN D AND E DECKS
Pictures by HUMPHREY SPENDER, A.R.I.B.A.

MAIN STAIRS BETWEEN E AND F DECKS
Pictures by BARBARA JONES

FLAT
Fabric Collages by KAYE PEMBERTON

DANCE SPACE
Fluorescent Mural by JOHN HUTTON

Left
List of artists and designers used on the Orcades III, available to passengers. Edward Bawden decorative border. *P&O Archives*

Come 1939, most passenger ships were requisitioned by their respective navies for wartime service, for the transportation of munitions, supplies and service personnel; the Orient Line were to lose the majority of its liners for such work. Post-war replacements saw Anderson and O'Rorke again in harness for *Orcades III* (1948) and *Oronsay II* (1951). Anderson had handed over some of the more technical aspects of these projects to his cousin and fellow director Ford Geddes. Holding on to the design side gave Anderson more scope and time to search for, and commission artists, undoubtedly aided by Clark.

As a result *Orcades III* was an altogether more 'arty' boat than her predecessors. The first class lounge was resplendent with British artists, much to Anderson's taste – modern but not too experimental. Much of the art aboard was essentially English in character (in spite of Anderson's tenet that design should never be nostalgic), with the likes of Edward Bawden, John Farleigh, Lynton Lamb, Kenneth Rowntree and Barbara Jones being commissioned. Jones, along with Rowntree, supplied pictures for a stairwell for which two sheets of glass were used, the lower one having a design on it, thus giving a three-dimensional effect. Commissioning the young John Minton and John Tunnard, involved rather more risk-taking – Tunnard perhaps being the most challenging artist used on the boat. And just as Beddington had done at Shell, Anderson was building up his own art collection by buying selectively from the artists he commissioned.

Marion Dorn, although having returned to America, still contributed designs for carpets and curtains for *Orcades III*, but a new generation of textile designers was being nurtured. The most extraordinary of these was Humphrey Spender, who had built up a considerable reputation as a photo-journalist, working for *Picture Post*, *Mass Observation* and the likes. By chance he had put in a design for a textile competition, won, and overnight, as it were, became a textile designer. He was part of Robin Darwin's new broom strategy at the Royal College of Art, and was to teach textiles there for some twenty years. Not surprisingly, he was somewhat daunted at taking over Dorn's mantle and

Laurence Scarfe 'Venetian Capriccio', Orcades III. *P&O Archives*

'English Garden Delights' 9-panel Mural by Edward Bawden for the Lounge of the Orcades III.

Douglas Annand working on mural for First Class Grill, Oronsay II. *P&O Archives*

Opposite
Douglas Annand painting the Kangaroo Hunt mural on the Orcades III, 1947. *National Gallery of Australia*

of being on display alongside her arch-modernist designs on the ship. However, he was soon to establish his own style and Anderson went on to use him on subsequent boats.

Bawden also contributed textiles to *Orcades III*. Although best remembered as a graphic artist and illustrator, he had been involved in textile design since the 1920s, working with the Calico Printers' Association, Footprints Ltd. and Edinburgh Weavers. In addition to curtains, Bawden also supplied a large mural for the first class lounge – 'English Garden of Delight' – consisting of nine vertical divisions crammed with ornamental terraces, greenhouses, pavilions and arbours, so typical of British immediate post-war nostalgia. It was Bawden who also provided a decorative edging to the card for passengers, which listed all the artists and designers involved. Anderson decided to have the card, presumably with an educational purpose, as well as it adding to the prestige of the Line.

Colour began to appear, certainly to a greater extent than with the refined muted tones of the two pre-war boats. Table tops for the Galleries were in blue, armchairs for the first class café in plum-coloured hide. And Anderson and O'Rorke began to make a really conscious effort to link designers' work to that of artists being hung. For example, John Hutton's carpets were made to reflect the colours in Bawden's mural and curtains. Anderson further developed his 'colonial' commissions on *Orcades III*. Particularly striking was Douglas Annand's relief 'Kangaroo Hunt', consisting of three panels using aboriginal motifs.

Oronsay II, the next liner, replaced her namesake that had been sunk within forty-eight hours of the sinking of *Orcades II*. An article in *Art and Industry* trumpeted the arrival of *Oronsay II*, the *Orcades III* sister ship, which went into service in 1951:

This latest addition to the Orient fleet is eminently worthy of the tributes that will undoubtedly be paid her. She is a triumphant

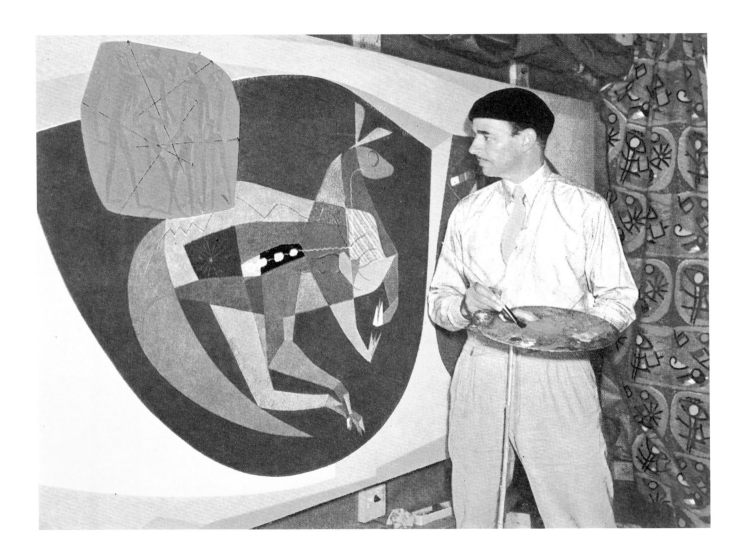

HAMPTON COURT PALACE

ORIENT LINE

 HIS is one of a series of six lithographs by Mr. Barnett Freedman of some of the historic palaces and buildings in or about London associated with the Royal Family

The lithographs in the series are: Buckingham Palace from the Mall; Tower of London, White Tower; Horse Guards; Windsor Castle, Norman Gate; Hampton Court Palace; St. James's Palace

Anyone wishing for a set to keep or send to friends can get one from the Head Saloon Steward or from the Managers of the Orient Line at 5 Fenchurch Avenue, London, E.C.3

Opposite and right
Menu Cards for the Orient Line,
two from a series of lithographs
by Barnett Freedman.

THE HORSE GUARDS, WHITEHALL.

Chapter I

Orlando Sails to the Arctic Regions.
(Chapter 3)

Opposite
From a series of 'Orlando' menu cards for the Orient Line by Kathleen Hale.

Right
Menu cover featuring Tower Bridge, designed by Clive Emanuel.

Right
List of artists and designers used on the Oronsay II. *P&O Archives*

Opposite
Information booklet, Oronsay II. *P&O Archives*

S.S. ORONSAY

PRINCIPAL DECORATIVE FEATURES

INTERIOR ARCHITECTURE
By BRIAN O'RORKE, R.A., F.R.I.B.A., R.D.I.

BALLROOM
By Messrs. GEORGE, TREW AND DUNN, *Chartered Architects*

THE TARGE & BROADSWORD BADGE
Designed by LYNTON LAMB, F.R.S.A., F.S.I.A.

THE GRILL
Decorative Panelling designed and executed by
DOUGLAS ANNAND
Carpet designed by DOUGLAS ANNAND

LOUNGE
Mural by EDWARD BAWDEN, C.B.E., R.A., R.D.I.
Curtains designed by EDWARD BAWDEN, C.B.E., R.A., R.D.I.
Carpet designed by HUMPHREY SPENDER, A.R.I.B.A.

GALLERIES
Carpets designed by HUMPHREY SPENDER, A.R.I.B.A.

TAVERN
Decorative Wall Panels by ROBERT MacBRYDE

RESTAURANT
Curtains designed by LOUIS LE BROCQUY, M.S.I.A.

CHILDREN'S & AUXILIARY DINING ROOMS
Glass Panel Decorations designed by
BARBARA JONES

MAIN STAIRCASE
Half Landings—
Flower Decorations designed and executed by
MRS. BARRY CRAIG

TOURIST CLASS RESTAURANT
Decorative Mirrors by
W. D. SUDDABY and C. E. FRYER

demonstration of enterprise on the part of her owners no less than skilful teamwork between designers, engineers, architects, artists and fitters and is an outstanding addition to the British Merchant Navy.[19]

In fact the *Oronsay II* seems much of a twin to *Orcades III*, employing many of the same artists and designers – Bawden, Lamb, Jones and Annand. Annand did a panel, 'Doodling', which Art and Industry described as 'delightful uninhibited gaiety', a term not previously applied to Orient Line design; additionally, the panel was to bring plastic aboard, a material to abound on subsequent boats. Apart from 'Doodling', the artwork aboard was, if anything, regressive, there being in the verandah bar what *Art and Industry* describe as 'a beautiful scale model of the clipper *Orient* (1853) surrounded by

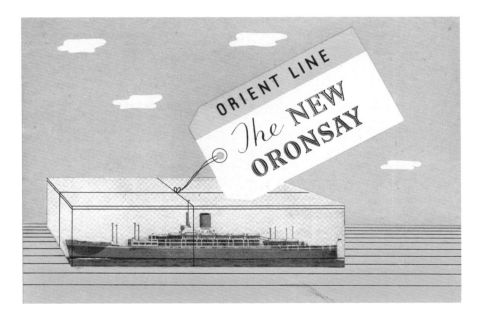

Humphrey Spender tromp l'oeil mural,
'The Boathouse Wall', Orsova.
P&O Archives

Opposite
Barbara Jones wall panels for
the Restaurant of the Orsova.

Right
Barbara Jones with Colin Anderson
in the bar of the Orsova.

prints of famous sailing ships suggesting the room of a retired sea captain!'

With the *Oronsay* the designers began to be faced with the problem of their increasing wide-open spaces having lower ceilings, presumably part of post-war economising with rationing still existing and industry still making the changes from munitions work. Such dimensions could bring feelings of oppression and consequently lighting design started to come to the fore in this and subsequent boats.

Humphrey Spender was again commissioned for textiles, and he was joined by Louis Le Brocquy, a designer and printer from Ireland who had recently come to London, and who was to teach alongside Spender at the RCA.

With the next liner, the *Orsova* (1954), Anderson and O'Rorke realised that the size and complexity of designing these post-war ships needed more than the

one-man band of O'Rorke's practice. He still carried overall responsibility, but John Wright was brought in for some of the public rooms, while George, Trew and Dunn designed the ballroom.

Although an appreciative article in the *Shipbuilding and Shipping Record* (May 1954) described the *Orsova* as 'uncompromisingly contemporary', there was a good deal of the furnishings and artwork that had been possibly tinged by the British parochial nostalgia of the Lion & Unicorn Pavilion of the Festival of Britain. There continued to be smooth surfaces, curved plain ceilings, unvarnished wood, slatted louvers, all definitely modernist features. But within this unadorned shell were murals and wall decorations that appeared incongruous. A particular talking point was Humphrey Spender's large *trompe l'oeil* for the first class lounge – 'The Boathouse' – which portrayed a miscellaneous mix of nautical oddments (flags, ropes, oil lamps, nets etc.) pegged on to rough wood planks.

Even less modernist was Barbara Jones' 'Scrapbook' for the first class restaurant. This literally consisted of scraps that she had taken from her immense collection of Victorian and Edwardian ephemera. Although her panels were technically advanced, warranting a good deal of correspondence with Bakelite, the images were hand shadows, taken from Cassels' *Book of Sports and Pastimes*, and, even less appropriate, pictures of artificial respiration, taken from a government pamphlet of 1894 entitled 'Inspiration in Dr. Silvester's Method'. With her rather edgy wit Jones considered these would be interesting topics of conversation for jaded travellers.

Another incongruity was the use of Windsor chairs in the tourist verandah bar, along with Ernest Race's up-to-the-minute deckchairs outside. Anderson and O'Rorke positively sought out a new approach to the standard deckchair and appreciating Race's experimenting with seating (he was at his most prolific in the 1950s and 60s) they were prepared to waive copyright in order to get what they wanted. The Neptune, as the chair was named, was to be used later on the *Oriana*. Race employed the same profile for both the seat

Opposite
Colin Anderson with an 'unsophisticated art' decorated pianola.

97

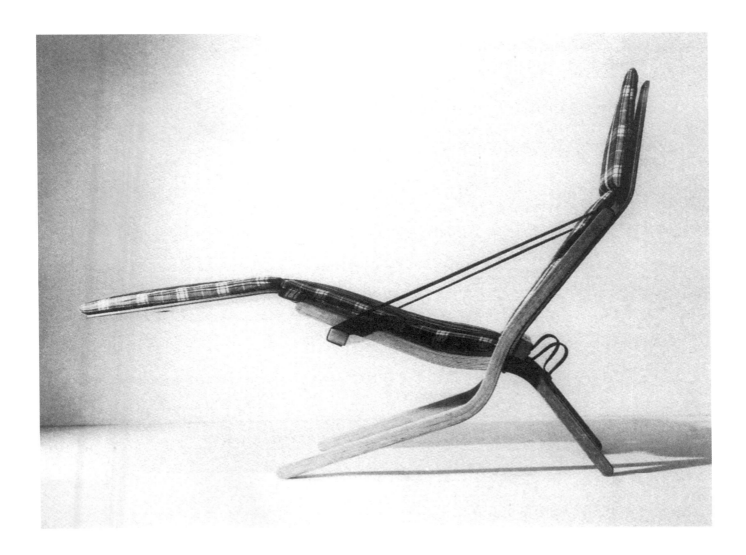

Below
Ceri Richards mural 'Vision of London' for
the First Class Restaurant of the Orsova.
Art & Heritage Services, Southampton

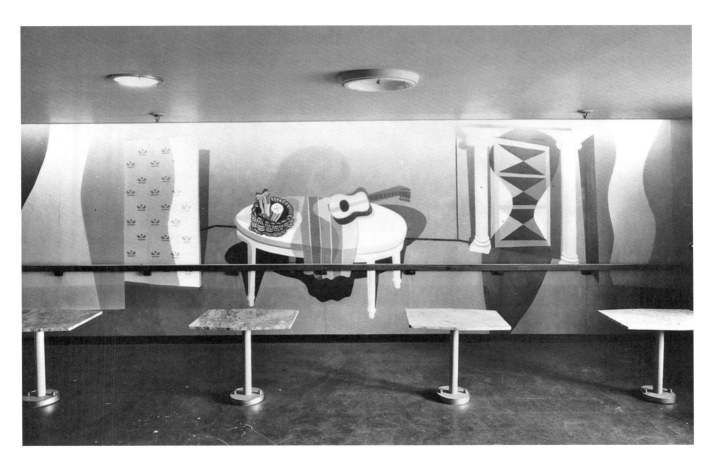

Misha Black of Design Research Unit,
design co-ordinator for the Oriana.
The Design Archives, University of Brighton

FANFARE FOR ORIANA

Children's Playroom of the Oriana with teak and aluminium climbing frame designed by Design Research Unit.

Opposite
Benjamin Britten's Fanfare for the launch of the Oriana.

and the back with consequent savings of cost. For each, a single mould of pre-formed plywood was used with a wide slot cut out of the back for a cushion to support the neck. To avoid using hinges, which tended to rust, the back-rest panel and front legs formed one assembly and the seat panel and rear legs another. Hazel Conway, considering the range of Race designs, wrote:

> To pinpoint a particular work of a designer as being his most original design is liable to raise more questions than it answers. Nevertheless, in terms of form, material and economy of solution to a particular problem, the Neptune stacking and folding chair could perhaps be considered as qualifying as one of Race's most original designs.[20]

Basil Marriott, in his article in the *Shipbuilding and Shipping Record*, rated the *Orsova* as highly modernistic:

> The keynote is simplicity, not of a deceptive kind, resulting from a discriminating whittling down and not from poverty of ideas. The elegance throughout is not a matter of added ornament; it results from a fastidious choice of materials, and skill in their use.[21]

It is not without significance that Anderson was appointed Chair of the RCA Council in 1952, for the *Oriana*, the last of the Orient Line liners, was to use a number of designers from the College. O'Rorke took on the role of consultant architect and the responsibility for the overall design policy and co-ordination was now given to the Design Research Unit (DRU). Although commissioned for the liner in 1956, by 1959 Misha Black, a director of DRU, had become Professor of Industrial Design at RCA. Along with the designers from DRU used on the *Oriana* were college worthies such as Professor R.Y. Gooden and Richard Russell (Professor of the School of Wood, Metals and Plastics). Gooden designed a chandelier, Russell and his partners were architects for the first class restaurant, and a number of young graduates from the College

(Brian Milne, Margaret Kaye, Barbara Bennett and Althea McNish) provided panels, murals, furniture and textiles.

In all four design groups were used (O'Rorke, DRU, R.D. Russell and Partners, and Ward & Austin). Black gave a justification for this (*SIA Journal*, January 1961) in that he felt that in the 'microscopic world' of the liner, variety was essential to beat the 'spectre of boredom'. That Black was closely following Anderson's 'fit for purpose' is exemplified by one

of his initial checklists noting such points as easy passenger circulation, atmosphere of well-being, public rooms light and airy with a tang of the sea, variation of design, and unobtrusive services. He set out DRU's general aim for the boat:

> The whole scheme of decoration must be sufficiently positive to give a definite personality to the ship equal to the individuality of its external form. The passenger should end his journey with positive pleasurable memories of the special world in which he has lived for days or weeks...[22]

Some thirty designers were used on the *Oriana*. Along with the new injection from DRU and RCA were designers from previous boats, including Humphrey Spender, Barbara Jones and Ernest Race. Race added his Cormorant and Tripos chairs to the Neptune. The Cormorant attracted much attention, won a number of design awards, and although originally planned as a deckchair for the Orient Line, it became a popular outdoor chair for domestic use. And the *Oriana* provided a showcase for another chair designer, Robin Day, who was experimenting with his plastic shell chairs at the time. And yet a further new wave of textile designers were commissioned, of which Marianne Straub was to become the best known. Three of her fabrics were chosen for the *Oriana* – 'Barfield', 'Munster' and 'Oriana Stripe'.

The murals and wall decorations were more in tune with the overall design than in the *Orsova*. Anderson commissioned John Piper to produce a large mural (4ft 8in x 25ft) for the Princess Room. The Andersons had met the Pipers through Clark and would visit them at Fawley Bottom, which Anderson described as 'jolly and rich a rustic, bohemian interior as you could imagine'. The mural was considered so outstanding it was hung in the P&O boardroom to be viewed by all the directors before being fixed on board. It was to serve as a screen – the mural facing the main part of the Princess Room, the reverse housing a library.

Olive Sullivan 'Masque of Oriana', Tourist Ballroom, Oriana. *Art & Heritage Services, Southampton*

Left
John Piper 'Landscape of Two Seasons'
mural for the Princess Room of the Oriana.
Art & Heritage Services, Southampton

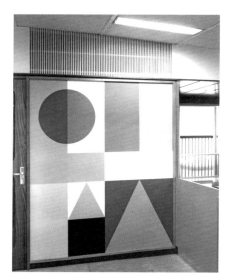

Robert Perritt mural for the First Class Junior Club, Oriana. *Art & Heritage Services Southampton*

Anderson had, for some time, been concerned about the difference between first- and second-class facilities and accommodation on Orient Line ships. In his Royal Society of Arts lecture (1966), he made his concern into a prediction:

> I believe the separation of the classes on board ship has been clung on to far too long and that the future lies in accommodating a much wider range of income groups within one class, sharing public facilities but enjoying a wide choice of cabin accommodation…[23]

By the time the *Oriana* was designed Anderson hadn't been fully able to achieve this, but with each successive post-war liner he had worked towards the attention to design for the tourist class becoming equal to that for the First; and Misha Black, who shared Anderson's values in this respect, attempted to provide an equal variety for both classes. Looking back on his first essay in designing for liners Misha Black recorded:

> At the end, when the *Oriana* sailed on her maiden voyage on 3 December those of us who had worked on her for over two years were left with mixed feelings. We had learned a lot about ships. We knew about sheer and camber and also that the central area of a modern ship is pretty rectangular … we have between the lot of us … produced a ship interior which is the best yet out of a British shipyard.[24]

The *Oriana* was the last boat in which Anderson took a really active interest, researching ideas for new cutlery, among other activities. He commissioned Benjamin Britten to compose a bugle call specifically for the boat, considering that such a contemporary contribution from another art would but reinforce the totally up-to-date character of the *Oriana*. Anderson was still very much an éminence gris, supervising every stage through weekly meetings with the design team. Misha Black was emphatic in declaring that Anderson had set the standard for them all, and that if any faults were found or criticisms made of

Barbara Jones 'Ocean Life' Warerite Panels, the Ocean Bar, Oriana.

Dorritt Dekk window display for 'P&O–Orient Lines'.

Dorritt Dekk entertainment programme covers. *P&O Archives*

'Float or Fly' Orient Line poster designed by
Dick Negus/Philip Sharland. *P&O Archives*

'Boomerang Trips' poster designed by John Bainbridge.
P&O Archives

Opposite John Bainbridge poster. *P&O Archives*

The Monarch of the Sea
First Lord of the Admiralty

the design they were definitely to be placed at the door of the designer and not of the client.

O'Rorke, looking back on their long partnership from a vantage point in 1966, summed up Anderson's contribution:

> Sir Colin Anderson is no armchair theorist about shipping. He must have spent a great many hours of his life in the shipbuilding yards and hours in the drawing office, really getting down to discussion of such varied things as glass-fibre lifeboats, baggage handling, and even the best way to serve cocktails in the bars. Many more hours have been spent in the sample cabins with fifteen or twenty people trying to decide how passengers will behave and how to cope with their eccentricities. In all of this he has been a tremendous help to the designers concerned. He has held the balance between them and the shipbuilders, he has encouraged them all the time, and in fact has been the real leader of the successive teams of designers. His work on passenger liners has had a side effect and very considerable influence in the improvement of standards of design in many shore-based industries, particularly in furniture and furnishings.[25]

Anderson and O'Rorke both were to claim the influence of their work, not only on other shipping lines but on design ashore as well. Although, perhaps with journalistic licence, the Society of Industrial Artists' newsletter (August 1951) declared that when the Orsova had been designed in that year it 'caused such a stir in shipbuilding circles that work has been stopped on at least one company's new ships on the stocks while the directors look again at the Jacobean panelling and the fluted pillars in the first class lounge – it doesn't look first class now'.

 Certainly other Australian routes began to commission artists, as with Ben Nicholson painting abstract murals for NZSS *Rangitane* (1950) and P&O using Kenneth Rowntree for the *Iberia*. And other lines also took up the idea of having 'good' art aboard to increase status, as Shaw Savill using Felix Kelly

Sir Hugh Casson, design architect Canberra. *National Portrait Gallery*

for their *Northern Star* (1962) and Union Castle also using him for their *Windsor Castle* (1960) and *Transvaal Castle* (1961). Even Dennis Lennon's designs for the QE2 (1969) were said to be 'developing the impetus' that Anderson had shown with the *Oriana* and *Canberra*.

On shore there was a direct influence in that O'Rorke also designed hotel interiors, for example, the Berkeley Hotel, London; aircraft interiors, such as Vickers v.c.1 Viking airliner; and trains, including three London, Midland & Scottish royal carriages for King George VI and Queen Elizabeth. And when Anderson commissioned Gollins Melvin & Ward to design new headquarters for P&O in Leadenhall Street in 1969 he had the shore architects working in teams with his version of modernism, just as he had had for his ships; and showed an equal supervision of detail down to demanding a shelf on which the receptionist could keep her sandwiches! In taking their modernist approach to such projects the two could certainly justify their claims, to an extent. That the design of the Orient Line ships, from the Orion to the *Oriana*, did not get the publicity and acclaim that it deserved, nor figure as large in the history of liner design as the Cunard's *Queens*, almost certainly can be put down to the lesser importance, politically and commercially, of the Far-Eastern routes to those of the transatlantic.

With the absorption of the Orient Line into P&O in 1960, Anderson remained an active director as far as shipping business was concerned, but had an altogether lesser involvement in design matters. Yet when Hugh Casson (who had been Director of Architecture at the Festival of Britain, and was, at the time, Professor of Interior Design at RCA) was commissioned to head the design team for P&O's *Canberra*, Anderson was still *the* authority to turn to. Casson, in spite of his considerable experience, was unsure as to how 'modern' the directors wanted the *Canberra* to be because, although the P&O had provided comfortable interiors for their own fleet they had, up to that time, no particular reputation for Modernism. Casson suggested to Sir Donald Anderson, Colin's brother and chairman of P&O, that a small sub-committee be appointed, to

Meridian Lounge, Canberra. *P&O Archive*

Crow's Nest, Canberra. *P&O Archives*

Tourist Cabin, Canberra. *P&O Archives*

Edward Ardizzone mural for the Children's Room of the Canberra. *P&O Archives*

include Board representatives, to choose or commission furnishings. Donald Anderson firmly replied to Casson that they were relying on *him* when it came to taste, albeit if one of the directors had a 'bright idea' they would pass it on to him. Sir Donald added:

> There is no one better fitted than my brother Colin to guide decisions on anything on which you want a ruling and he will be glad to do so … You are responsible for choosing and Colin for authorising.[26]

Although the *Canberra* made use of some of the Orient Line designers, such as John Wright and Ernest Race, and still made 'function for purpose' a prime consideration, it was altogether a more frivolous, jolly, colourful boat, steering a design path between the spiky crystallographic forms of the Festival of Britain and the Pop Art developments happening at the RCA. The light-heartedness of the *Canberra* compares favourably with the more self-conscious splendour of the QE2. When James Gardner was questioned about the design of the QE2 by the shipping historian Philip Dawson, he actually admitted that their designs set out to pander to the wealthy Americans, who were likely to make up the bulk of the passengers and for whom 'Bauhaus' style would just not do. Dawson considered that although the QE2 was altogether more luxurious than the *Canberra*, the latter actually had some more sophisticated designs.

Paradoxically, by the time British designers were making their mark on the interior of liners, and had achieved status vis-à-vis shipping companies and shipbuilders, the vessels themselves were becoming dinosaurs. In 1927 Charles F. Lindburgh flew the Spirit of St. Louis from New York to Paris. In October 1958 a commercial jet crossed the North Atlantic for the first time. The increasing supremacy of air travel forced the shipping companies to turn to full-time cruising and, with this, the trend was for medium-sized ships with their design regressing to a common mean for one-class holidaying; the glory days of the ocean liner were over.

Left and opposite
Ruskin Spears decorative panels for the
Cricketers Tavern, Canberra. Featuring
cricketers Ranjitsinhji, Grace and Bradman.
P&O Archives

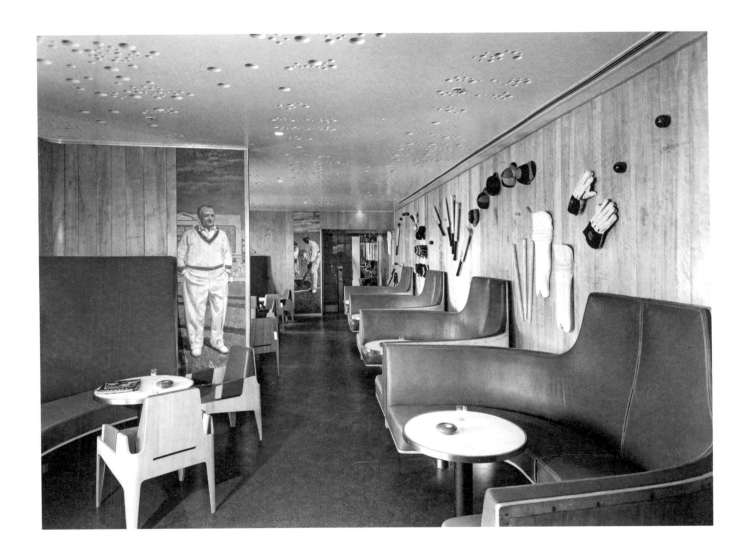

Tableware designed by Lady Casson for the Canberra. *P&O Archives*

Conran chair, Canberra. *P&O Archives*

Grill Room & Bar of the QE2. *Art & Heritage Services, Southampton*

Cabin Class Foyet of the QE2. *Art & Heritage Services, Southampton*

COLIN ANDERSON ASHORE

Anderson's obituary in *The Times* (17 October 1980) suggested that he had been rather overshadowed in the family business by his brilliant, and more formidable, elder brother, Donald, an accountant with a lesser interest in design. But Colin Anderson was no slouch when it came to shipping, becoming a director of P&O, while Donald was chairman. And, following family tradition for public service, Anderson took responsibilities beyond the company, becoming, at various times, chairman of the London Port Employers and of the National Association of Port Employers, President of the Seaman's Hospital Society, Prime Warden of the Fishmongers' Company, President of the Chamber of Shipping and Hon. President of the International Chamber of Shipping.

But it was within the art world ashore that Anderson was to become a really significant figure. Clark, in his memoirs 'The Other Half', wrote of Anderson ashore:

> With the exception of David Crawford, Colin did more for the arts than anyone in England … He became Chairman of the Royal Fine Arts Commission, Chairman of the English Opera Group, Chairman of the Tate Gallery, Chairman of the Royal College of Art, Chairman of the Contemporary Art Society and the National Council of Design, Trustee of the Gulbenkian Foundation … Let no one suppose such chairmanships are a sinecure like certain City directorships … I am sure that he did not draw a penny of income from any of these offices and they gave him no added status or power. They were done out of a devotion to the public interest…[27]

(David Crawford, Lord Crawford, had been a politician but became a writer on art and a member of various committees and trusteeships connected to the arts.) Clark's list was by no means exhaustive, as among Anderson's other 'contributions to the Arts' were his Presidency of the Design and Industries Association, his membership of the Design Panel of British Rail, his work for

the City Arts Trust, his acting as Trustee for Covent Garden Opera Company, and his appearance as judge for various competitions and prizes (as for the Duke of Edinburgh's Design Prize). When Anderson retired to Jersey he wrote to Clark, 'I am giving up all my pompous offices' – a confirmation of what Clark had appraised Anderson's motivation to be.

From the earliest days of Anderson's essays in the design of ships' interiors, he had personally encouraged artists he particularly admired. He not only gave them commissions and bought their work, he actually gave them financial help as well. Graham Sutherland, whom Anderson had met via Clark, was a favourite and wrote of his gratitude to Anderson:

> I do thank you for being literally the only one of my earliest supporters who follows what I am trying to do as I try to do it, naturally, and without slight prompting on my part.[28]

Looking back on his life Anderson wrote, 'I feel very happy when I think that I know and am known by Graham and Henry (Moore) ... I am very grateful to be seeing their development, and for that I feel not unwilling to forego other joys'.

For Ceri Richards, Anderson provided a small house in Alphamstone, Suffolk, as a refuge from London bombing during the war. He remained loyal in his admiration for Richards. Anderson's sensitivity to art, and fluency in expressing his aesthetic ideas, are clear from the lines he wrote in honour of Ceri Richards for Fischer Fine Art's 'Homage to Ceri Richards' exhibition catalogue in 1972:

> Beyond being the most steady friend, Ceri had the extra quality of being at the same time a fount of visual pleasures and surprises. It was an uncommon admixture of quiet efficiency with an intense poetic reaction to outsize stimuli. Few painters can have been more inspired by music and poetry than he – but then, he could equally have made a career in music. This range of responsiveness explains the width of stylistic variation within his total work. He never dreamed of denying the inspiration he had from other artists. He honoured them too much for that and, besides, he transmuted these experiences so that the resulting works flew unmistakably on strong, Ceri-given wings.[29]

Anderson's help for the two Roberts, Colquhoun and MacBryde, was extraordinary. During the 1930s the Andersons had moved to Bedford Place, and in 1941 the Roberts had become neighbours in nearby artists' studios. When the pair were at a very low ebb Anderson paid their rent, provided them with an account at their art suppliers, and later, when they had been burgled, bought them new furnishings for their flat. Sympathetic to their plight he put in a personal plea to the Artists' General Benevolent Society. In gratitude Colquhoun was to give Anderson some of his pictures.

The Andersons were eventually to build up a collection to rival that of the Clark's, including works by John Craxton, Barbara Hepworth, Ben Nicholson, Henry Moore, David Jones, Wyndham Lewis, Matthew Smith, Francis Bacon, Prunella Clough and Lucien Freud, as well as Sutherland and Richards – a roll call of 20th-century British art. For the catalogue of the 1950 Tate Gallery exhibition of Seventeen Collectors, of which Anderson was one, he shows something of the charm and enthusiasm of his personality in describing collector's motivation:

> Pure admiration; weakness; love of carved frames; friendship; nostalgia; snobbery; distaste for bare walls; greed of gain – all are possible, and some are respectable reasons for acquiring a picture. My wife and I confess to more than one of them, but we aim at the first ... We also find house-room for the unfashionable qualities of light-heartedness, of prettiness, and even of frivolity.[30]

The Anderson's were inveterate collectors, Anderson tracing it back to his pebble collecting on the beach at Aldeburgh as a child. In 1946 they moved to Admiral's House in Hampstead, near the Clarks, who were living in Upper Terrace House. Admiral's House had been built in 1700 and had featured in several of Constable's paintings. Its name was merely a coincidence to Anderson's shipping career, for no Admiral had lived there and it was only so named in 1917.

In spite of Anderson originating Modernism on to British ships, there were but a few remnants of Modernism to their furnishing of the house. It was very grand in construction and furnished accordingly. The dining room was described as particularly striking with Regency furniture, appropriate to the period of the house, shoulder-to-shoulder, perhaps inappropriately, to a large Matthew Smith nude, a Sutherland landscape and a farm scene by Frances Hodgkin.

The most integrated room was at the top of the house and this was devoted to Victoriana – knick-knacks and curiosities, à la Barbara Jones, alongside a collection of Pre-Raphaelite paintings, one of the most splendid being Holman Hunt's *The Awakening Conscience*, which Anderson was later to give to the Tate Gallery. In his house in Jersey he was to keep to Victorian and Edwardian furnishings declaring, 'we will smother the walls with our pictures, and the tables with our sculpture and objects' – gone was Bauhaus functionalism!

It was as late as 1960 that the Andersons started collecting what were to become their most renowned furnishings. They began their Art Nouveau collection with pieces by Alphonse Mucha and Emile Galle; but, at the other end of the scale, sought pieces out in bric-a-brac shops and from market stalls. They were much encouraged in this by Anderson's cousin, Margaret Geddes, who had married Prince Ludwig of Hesse and lived near Dormstadt, which had been a major centre for the style. Through Margaret they met K.A. Citroen, one of the most important collector's of Art Nouveau, who became the Andersons' friend and advisor, even giving them pieces from his own collection. All this was at a time when the style was not at all fashionable. Their collecting enthusiasm was such that in the nine years between 1962 and 1971 they had accumulated what was considered the finest collection in England.

In 1976, when the Andersons planned to leave England for Jersey, where the family had property, they decided to put their collection on show for the public, and when space could not be found by the National Trust, Anderson, hearing of Sir Robert and Lady Sainsbury's plans for an art centre and art history faculty at the University of East Anglia, approached them on the matter. In 1978 the collection was gifted to the centre.

In the catalogue to The Anderson Collection, Anderson writes charmingly of the growth and wane of his collecting habit:

> The human instinct for collecting things is inborn. The infant starts collecting stones and from these it is only a toddle through bus tickets to pressed flowers and from them onwards by way of postage stamps and Toby jugs, to the last stages of first editions, classical gold coins

and paintings by Vermeer. I have already been through a gamut, on a scale considerably lower in tone than the one I have sketched, and, having passed my peak, and now set on my downward path, having detected in myself a renewal of my former attachment to pebbles, complemented by a growing horror of postage stamps and a strange feeling of indifference to bus tickets.[31]

Of the many art organisations with which Anderson was associated, his time at the Tate Gallery was perhaps most turbulent and headline-catching. He was vice-chairman of the Trustees from 1953 and chairman from 1960. Frances Spalding has provided one of the most comprehensive accounts of the Tate Affair – a sorry morality tale of human vanity, duplicity and sheer pettiness. Suffice it to say that when Anderson took up his vice-chairmanship he found himself in the middle of intrigues and vendettas revolving around the directorship of John Rothenstein that must have made his wrestling with manufacturers and shipbuilders seem merely spots of bother, or lover's tiffs, soon mended. The chief adversaries in the drama were Douglas Cooper, Herbert Read, Graham Sutherland, Humphrey Brooke and the arch-villain of the piece, the South African artist and Tate Keeper, Le Roux Smith Le Roux. Anderson wrote of him: 'Le Roux made me able, for ever more, to believe in Iago'. The saga, too complex, and indeed too petty to recount here, had the elements of the absurd (Zsa Zsa Gabor kicking her leg up on a Tate exhibit) to sheer mismanagement if not fraud (the handling of the Chantry Bequest and of the Knapping Fund). Suffice it to say that by the time Anderson arrived on the scene the Trustees were considering sacking both Rothenstein and Le Roux.

Spalding does not specify Anderson's role in the 'Tate Affair', but just as his tactfulness and diplomacy and practicality had been effective in holding sway between designers and shipbuilders with such creative results, he seems to have exerted a similar influence at the Tate. Certainly several meetings of Trustees and sub-Cabals of Trustees took place in the Pre-Raphaelite room

Anderson with Robin Darwin and the Queen Mother. *Royal College of Art, Archives*

in Admiralty House during February of 1954, a time that Spalding describes as the most dramatic in the Tate's history. As a result of such meetings Le Roux departed, the Tate got its own Accounts Department and Rothenstein remained, but was eventually asked to resign in 1964. Anderson was also a prime mover in persuading the Treasury that the Tate needed to fill the considerable gaps in its modern foreign collection; and as a result of his efforts the Treasury came up with an additional fifty thousand pounds for five years, which enabled the purchasing of some Picasso's and of the iconic Matisse – *The Snail*.

Anderson's association with the Royal College of Art (RCA) was even longer than with the Tate, and even more challenging. At the end of the Second World War the state and status of the RCA was questionable, and in 1948 Robin Darwin took up the reins to attempt to reshape the college. His 'new-brooming' involved many of the older teaching staff being ousted with undue haste, followed by an influx of young blood. Darwin was determined to obtain public and private commissions for the college and to attract the maximum of publicity thereby. A major vehicle for this was the College Council, which he packed with key personalities. Anderson was courted for the Council, along with the likes of Jack Beddington, Geoffrey Dunn (of the Good Furniture Group), Sir Michael Balcon (Head of Ealing Film Studios), Sir Francis Meynell (of the Nonesuch Press), and, perhaps with greatest influence, Gordon Russell (director of the relatively newly established Council of Industrial Design). Darwin would not have been disappointed with Anderson's appointment, for he obtained commissions for both staff and students for the Orient Line and P&O boats, particularly for the *Oriana* and the *Canberra*.

Two major challenges faced Darwin, beyond re-establishing the college's reputation generally. The first was to obtain purpose-built premises, as several sites were then being occupied; the second was to gain for the college university status, by which it could award its own qualifications. It is said that

Anderson's low-key diplomacy and natural charm did much to ease the way
for both these projects, as Darwin was an altogether more volatile character.
By the time Anderson was appointed first Provost for the college in 1967 both
of Darwin's projects had been successful.

The Times, reporting the ceremony for the first Provost, at which Anderson
additionally conferred an honorary degree on the Duke of Edinburgh,
not only gives a delightful thumbnail sketch of Anderson, but also hints at
Darwin's temperament:

> Sir Colin Anderson, who seems somehow to remain unspoiled by
> his unfair share of good looks, charm and money, looked superb as
> first Provost and made a characteristic well-turned speech in which

149

he referred to the Vice-Provost, Sir Robin Darwin, as a particularly powerful and resilient piece of equipment, of truest steel, and apt to uncoil rapidly…[32]

An altogether more straightforward design-related undertaking, with far-reaching practical consequences, was Anderson's appointment as chairman of a Department of Transport committee set up in 1957 to get new road signs for a network of motorways that were then being planned. Many road signs had been removed during the Second World War, for reasons of security in case of a Nazi invasion. Other existing signs dated back to 1933, some as far back as 1904. Anderson had read of the successful signing work at Gatwick Airport carried out by Jock Kinneir and had commissioned him to provide a baggage labelling system for P&O. Kinneir seemed, to Anderson, the obvious choice for the motorways assignment. All aspects of road signing were researched, drawing from European and American practice, ideas tested, initial on-site trialling taking place on the Preston Bypass. Kinneir, and his partner Margaret Calvert, developed a new typeface for their signs – 'Transport' – based on Akzidenz Grotesk. The Anderson Report (1962) not only recommended the adoption of this, as it had proved effective at being read at speed, but also that the letters should stand out against a blue background.

The results were considered so successful that a further committee under Sir Walter Worboys was set up to review signage on all other roads and Kinneir was again appointed the designer. Kinneir and Calvert went on to produce a typeface for British Rail and for further airports. Anderson's effective handling of designers at sea was echoed in his handling of them ashore, with similar cascading results.

Anderson's association with the Design Council began in 1951. Besides being a member, he would frequently be called upon to chair their committees, as for the annual design awards. The Council greatly valued Anderson's contributions and, it is thought, would have liked to have involved him a great deal more, even as director, but his workload and his other voluntary activities precluded this.

As chairman of the Contemporary Art Society (1956–60) Anderson gave considerable support to their first female secretary, Pauline Vogelpoel, in her establishing herself in what was largely a man's world; and again Admiral's House was to feature, this time in 'treats for members'.

Although Clark declared that Anderson carried out these many, various, and overlapping services for no personal gain, his contributions to art and design attracted much acclaim and recognition. He was knighted in 1950 and received a KBE; but Anderson would have been equally pleased with the recognition he got from academic and professional bodies concerned with art and design – a Doctor of Law from Aberdeen University; an Honorary Membership of the Royal Institute of British Architects; becoming the first Provost of RCA; being the first recipient of the Royal Society of Arts Bicentenary Medal given to Anderson 'as a director of a steamship company, has maintained a strong policy for the improvement of the design of new ships'. All of this would have validated Anderson's aesthetic talents and values that he had chosen to keep hidden at Oxford, but which, through his career, had become public knowledge.

On his retirement from his Tate responsibilities in 1967, Adrian Stokes, one of the senior trustees, in a tribute to Anderson, neatly summed up the nicely balanced qualities that made him so effective as the man who managed teams of designers, afloat and ashore, influenced the careers of artists, and ran so many public committees concerned with art and design:

Sensitivity with a practical imagination, firmness with tolerance and elasticity, and great kindness with dispatch.[33]

Anderson well earned his inclusion in the Pantheon of Foot-note Men.

CHRONOLOGY

1904	Born in London
1917–22	Eton
1922–25	Trinity College, Oxford
1925	Joined Anderson, Green & Co.
1930	Junior director, Anderson, Green & Co.
1932	Married Morna MacCormick (d. of Sir Alexander MacCormick)
1935	*Orion*
1937	*Orcades II*
1948	*Orcades III*
1950	Knighted
1951	First recipient of the Royal Society for the Arts Bicentenary Medal
1951	Elected to the Council of Industrial Design
1951	*Oronsay II*
1952	On Council of Royal College of Art (RCA)
1953	Awarded Hon. Des. RCA
1953–67	Vice-Chairman, the Chairman (1960) of the Trustees of the Tate Gallery
1954	Awarded Jubilee Medal (RSA)
1954	*Orsova*
1960	*Oriana*
1967	First Provost RCA
1968–76	Chairman of the Royal Fine Arts Commission
1969	KBE
1978	Anderson's collection of Art Nouveau donated to the Sainsbury Centre for the Arts, University of East Anglia
1980	Died Jersey

REFERENCES

1 Colin Skelton Anderson, *Three Score Years & Ten*, 1974
2 as [1]
3 as [1]
4 Sir Colin Anderson, 'Ship Interiors', P&O house magazine, June 1969
5 Alan Powers, 'Travelling in Style', *The Spectator*, May 1986
6 Exhibition catalogue, 'The Ocean Liner', Cooper Hewitt Museum, NY
7 as [4]
8 Uwe Westphal, 'The Bauhaus', Studio Editions, 1991
9 Barbara Wadsworth, 'Edward Wadsworth', Michael Russell, 1989
10 as [4]
11 Veronica Sekules, 'The Ship-owner as patron: Sir Colin Anderson and the Orient Line 1930–1966', *Journal of the Decorative Art Society*, 1986
12 The Orion', *Shipbuilding and Shipping Record*, 26 December 1935
13 Colin Anderson, 'McKnight Kauffer', *Advertising Review*, vol. 1, 1954
14 as [1]
15 David McKee
16 *Orcades II* ship's brochure
17 Sir Colin Anderson, 'The Interior Design of Passenger Ships', *Journal of the Royal Society of Arts*, May 1966
18 Clive Bell, quoted in Neil Potter & Jack Frost, 'The Queen Mary', George G. Harrap, 1971
19 'The New Oronsay', *Art and Industry*, September 1951
20 Hazel Conway, 'Ernest Race', *The Design Council*, 1982
21 Basil Marriott, 'The Orsova Decorations', *Shipbuilding and Shipping Record*, May 1954

22   Avril Blake, 'Misha Black', *The Design Council*, 1984

23   as [17]

24   Misha Black, 'Oriana Coordinated', *SIA Journal*, 1961

25   as [17]

26   Sir Donald Anderson to Hugh Casson [note] P&O archives

27   Kenneth Clark, 'The Other Half', Harper & Row, 1977

28   Anderson to Clark [letter], The Tate Gallery Archives 1.2.74

29   Colin Anderson in 'Homage to Ceri Richards', Fischer Fine Art, 1972

30   Colin Anderson in catal., 'The Private Collector', Tate Gallery, 1950

31   catal., 'The Anderson Collection of Art Nouveau', Sainsbury Centre for the Visual Arts, University of East Anglia

32   RCA archives [undated]

33   Frances Spalding, 'The Tate, a history', Tate Gallery Publishing, 1998

ACKNOWLEDGEMENTS

My mainstay throughout – Susie Cox, P&O Art Curator.

My thanks to the following archivists/librarians and their colleagues, who gave me time, interest, generosity and efficiency, within the oft times straightened circumstances in which they work:

The Cunard Archive, Sydney Jones Library, University of Liverpool
The Design Archives, Faculty of Arts and Architecture, Brighton University
The Picture Library, National Maritime Museum, Greenwich
The Photographic Archives, Liverpool Maritime Museum
Royal College of Art Archive
RIBA British Architectural Library
The Tate Gallery Archives
V&A Design Archives
Warner Textile Archive

And I am also grateful to the many dealers in shipping books and ephemera who have shared their enthusiasms and knowledge.